Smoking

Sarah Ridley

W

FRANKLIN WATTS
LONDON•SYDNEY

This edition published in 2011 by Franklin Watts

338 Euston Road, London NW1 3BH

Franklin Watts Australia

Level 17/207 Kent Street

Sydney, NSW 2000

Series editor: Melanie Palmer

Designed by: Pewter Design Associates

Series design: Peter Scoulding

ISBN 978 0 7496 9593 4

How Can I Be Healthy? Smoking is a reduced text version of *It's Your Health: Smoking*.
The original text was by Judith Anderson.

Illustration: Mike Atkinson and Guy Smith, Mainline Design

Picture researcher: Diana Morris

Series consultant: Wendy Anthony, Health Education Unit, Education Service, Birmingham City Council

Picture credits:

Jerry Arcieri/Corbis: 8c. Paul Baldesare/Photofusion. Posed by models: front cover. Baumgartner Olivia/Corbis Sygma: 41cr. Norm Betts/Rex Features: 33bl. Richard Bickel/Corbis: 8bl. Ed Bock/Corbis: 20b. BSIP, Alexandre/SPL: 23c. BSIP, Laurent/SPL: 21b. Alexander Caminada/Rex Features: 24c. Mark Clarke/SPL: 11tr. Stuart Clarke/Rex Features: 25b. Pablo Corral/Corbis: 30t. Deep Light/SPL:19t. Colin Edwards/Photofusion: 34t. Chris Fairclough: 4, 9, 14, 36, 41, 45. Owen Franken/Corbis: 16b. A. Glauberman/SPL:18c. Paul Hardy/Corbis: 17b. Hayley Madden/S.I.N/Corbis: 40c. Faye Norman/SPL: 22c. Claire Paxton & Jacqui Farrow/SPL: 26c. Mark Peterson/Corbis: 29b, 31b. Harvey Pincis/SPL: 12c. James Prince/SPL: 35c. Joel W. Rogers/Corbis: 28b. Saturn Stills/SPL: 37t. Chuck Savage/Corbis: 39c. Christopher Smith/Corbis: 23b. Roman Soumar/Corbis: 29t. Stapleton Collection, UK/Bridgeman Art Library: 10b. Tom Stewart/Corbis: 38c. James A. Sugar/Corbis: 21c. Swim Ink/Corbis: 11b. Charles Sykes/Rex Features: 32b. Tek Image/SPL: 13bl. Jonathan Torgovnik/Corbis: 27t. Nik Wheeler/Corbis: 31t. Richard Young/Rex Features: 15c.

The Publisher would like to thank the Brunswick Club for Young People, Fulham, London for their help with this book. Thanks to our models, including Elliott Scott, Stevie Waite and Eva Webb.

Franklin Watts is a division of Hachette Children's Books, an Hachette UK company.
www.hachette.co.uk

Contents

What is tobacco?

Tobacco is made from the dried leaves of the tobacco plant. It is grown in more than 100 countries around the world. It is used in a variety of products including cigarettes, cigars, pipe tobacco, 'chew' tobacco and snuff powder.

There are over a billion cigarette smokers in the world.

Cigarettes

Cigarettes are made from dried tobacco, paper, additives and, in most cases, a filter. The filter helps to remove some of the tar from the cigarette smoke.

▲ Tobacco farmers have to use many pesticides on their crops in order to bring in a good harvest.

Your experience

"I hate the fact that my parents smoke. I know it is bad for their health and it makes our house and car stink."

Sam, aged 12

Why are cigarettes addictive?

The tobacco in cigarettes contains nicotine. Nicotine is one of the most addictive drugs in the world. This means that smokers quickly come to depend on it. Strangely, it does not have the same effect on everyone – some people find that it relaxes them, others that it gives them a boost of energy.

Chemicals and additives

Cigarettes contain over 4,000 chemicals as well as nicotine. Some occur naturally in tobacco but others are added. These chemicals help to keep the tobacco fresh and to mask any unpleasant taste or smell.

Oral tobacco

Not all tobacco users smoke cigarettes. In India, parts of Africa and Southeast Asia, people chew the dried leaves. It has also become popular in the USA. The chewing releases the flavour and the rest is spat out. People who use oral tobacco are far more likely to develop cancers in the mouth.

Your view

Smoking is addictive and it is one of the worst things that you can do for your health. It causes lung cancer, lung disease, heart disease, tooth decay and many other health problems. So why do you think so many people still smoke? Do they think it makes them look cool and grown-up?

Many people take up smoking when they are young.

The history of smoking

Historians believe that Native Americans were the first people to smoke tobacco. Travellers and explorers brought it from the Americas to Europe at the end of the 15th century.

Snuff, cigars and cigarettes

At first tobacco was smoked in pipes, but by the end of the 17th century some people were sniffing powdered tobacco, called 'snuff'. Cigars became fashionable amongst the wealthy in the 19th century, and then came the cigarette.

The 20th century

Cigarettes became increasingly popular after the invention of machines that could make thousands a day. The price dropped and they were no longer something that only rich people could afford. By the outbreak of

A wealthy woman is being offered snuff, powdered tobacco, in this 18th century painting.

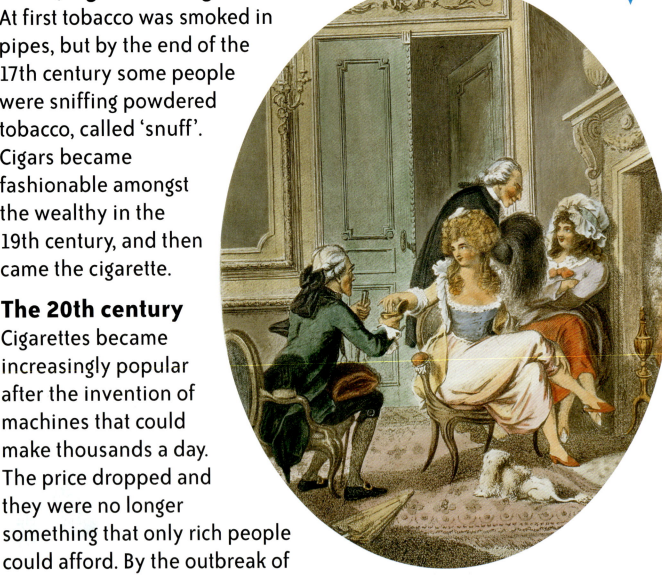

the First World War in 1914, smoking was a habit enjoyed by many men.

During the Second World War, US soldiers were given cigarettes as part of their rations. By the 1940s, about 65% of men and 41% of women in the UK were smokers.

Your experience

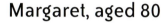

"When I was a girl, everyone smoked. People didn't realise the dangers. I've lasted this long and I am not going to give up now."

Margaret, aged 80

"SEND SMOKES TO SAMMY!"

"FIFTY-FIFTY ON MY LAST SMOKE, BILL!"

Mail Your Contributions to

"OUR BOYS IN FRANCE TOBACCO FUND"

West 44th Street   Endorsed by   New York City
                        War Department

▲ A First World War poster asks Americans to support the troops by sending them cigarettes.

Then came the clear evidence, during the 1950s, that smoking caused lung cancer. The powerful tobacco industry tried to deny this link at first. But the health message started to make a difference and, since the 1960s, smoking rates among adults in wealthy countries have generally declined. However, in many poorer countries in Asia and Africa, smoking is on the increase.

Your view

It was the fashion to smoke in the past but why do you think people continue to start smoking when they know the risks?

Smoke in your body

When someone smokes a cigarette, they pull smoke down into their lungs. From there, chemicals in the smoke are absorbed into the bloodstream and travel to all parts of the body.

Tobacco smoke contains over 4,000 chemicals. Many are present in tiny amounts, but they can still cause cancer.

In the lungs

When the tobacco smoke passes down into the lungs it irritates the delicate lining of the air passages. This may make people cough or experience a burning feeling. The tar in the smoke sticks to the lungs and can cause cancer. It also makes it more difficult for the lungs to fight colds, coughs and flu.

Your experience

"The first time I smoked it was awful. I thought my throat was on fire and I felt sick. I got used to it though and I liked the buzz it gave me."

Jack, aged 18

In the bloodstream

Once the chemicals from tobacco smoke get into the bloodstream, they travel around the body. Carbon monoxide, one of the chemicals, reduces the blood's ability to carry oxygen. This makes the heart and lungs have to work harder to get enough oxygen round the body. Within seconds of smoking, nicotine, another chemical, reaches the brain. There it raises the heart rate and blood pressure and generates feelings of pleasure.

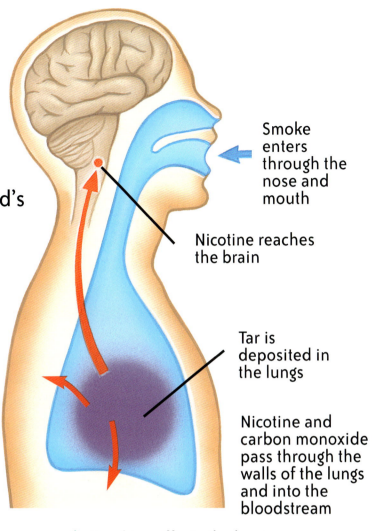

Smoke enters through the nose and mouth

Nicotine reaches the brain

Tar is deposited in the lungs

Nicotine and carbon monoxide pass through the walls of the lungs and into the bloodstream

▲ Smoking affects the lungs, blood and brain.

▼ Special machines 'smoke' cigarettes to test their chemical content.

It's your life

Smoking also causes changes in the smoker's blood. It makes it more 'sticky', causing fat to build up on the walls of the blood vessels. This leads to heart disease. Will you smoke now that you know it causes cancer, heart disease and breathing problems?

Starting to smoke

Many people start to smoke when they are teenagers, for several different reasons.

Rebelling and growing up

Children and teenagers can give several reasons why they start to smoke. Some are rebelling against their parents or against school rules. Others see smoking as something glamorous and grown-up that they want to do. Some people smoke because it makes them more confident in party situations.

Family and friends

Children are more likely to smoke if both of their parents smoke. They are also much more likely to start smoking if their brother, sister, best-friend or friendship group takes up the habit. Although it is natural for people to want to fit in with others, it is worth protecting your health by saying 'no' to cigarettes.

Friends and siblings can encourage others to smoke. ▼

Your experience

▶ "I go into town every Saturday with a group of friends from school. They all smoke, but at first I didn't want to. Now I've joined in as I don't want to be left out."

Emma, aged 14

It's your life

▶ Are you rebellious? It is normal to try to break away from your parents as you grow up. The problem is that if you start to smoke to shock your parents, you may be left with an addiction to cigarettes that is hard to break.

▲ Some young people are influenced by photos of stars smoking.

Influence of the media

Films, television, music and adverts are very good at creating an image of a lifestyle that we would like to share. Some researchers believe that when film stars or pop musicians smoke it encourages children to take up the habit in order to be like the stars.

Addiction

People continue to smoke for one reason only — they are addicted to nicotine. An addiction is when someone feels they cannot live without something. They depend on it to feel normal.

Just seven cigarettes

Recent research has shown that children who smoke as little as seven cigarettes a month can become addicted to nicotine.

The nicotine effect

When the drug nicotine reaches the brain, it triggers the release of dopamine – a chemical that gives off feelings of pleasure. Once the feeling wears off, the smoker wants another cigarette. Without the next cigarette, the smoker starts to feel restless and irritable, feelings that only go away by smoking.

It's your life

Nicotine is one of the most addictive drugs in the world. Will you take the risk of experimenting with smoking or will you decide it isn't worth the risk of becoming addicted?

Many young people ignore the risks of smoking.

Habit-forming

Smoking is often referred to as a 'habit', and this too is a form of addiction. The brain learns to link having a cigarette with certain situations or activities, such as watching TV or talking to friends. In some jobs, taking a 'smoke break' is the normal thing to do. This can make it difficult to give up smoking.

Your experience

"I've been smoking since I was 15. My urge to smoke is triggered by all sorts of things like stress and tiredness, or eating or relaxing. Even talking about smoking makes me want a cigarette."

Paul, aged 43

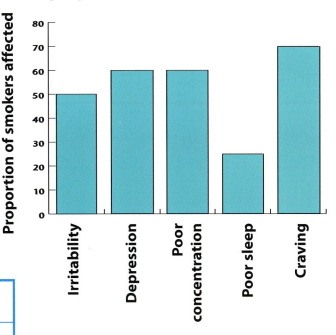

Symptoms of addiction to nicotine: proportion of smokers affected

Proportion of smokers affected

Symptoms of addiction to nicotine

Symptoms of addiction to nicotine

The craving for a cigarette can make it difficult to concentrate. Having another cigarette may seem like the only solution. And recent research suggests that nicotine can affect the developing brains of teenage smokers, making it hard for them to hear and understand what is being said to them. For help on quitting smoking, see pages 36–37.

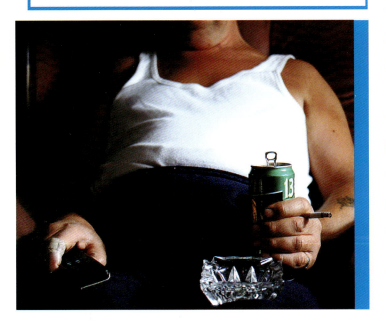

◄ Drinking alcohol and watching TV make some people reach for their cigarettes.

Smoking and disease

Most people know that smoking is bad for health. Yet young people continue to take up smoking. Many believe that they will have given up before they have harmed themselves.

Non-fatal diseases

Smokers are more likely to suffer from a wide range of illnesses such as impotence, psoriasis, hearing problems, coughs, chest pains and gum disease.

Cancer

Cigarette smoke contains cancer-causing chemicals. Many are absorbed in the mouth, throat and lungs which is why smokers suffer more from these types of cancer. But it also increases the risk of other cancers, including cancer of the bladder, kidneys and stomach.

The smoker's lung, right, is darker and shows damage. The non-smoker's lung, left, is smoother and paler.

Heart disease and strokes

A smoker is two to three times more likely to have a heart attack than a non-smoker. Nicotine raises blood pressure, forcing the heart to work harder. Carbon monoxide affects the ability of the blood to carry oxygen, also making the heart have to beat faster. Smoking thickens the walls of blood vessels, increasing the risk of a heart attack or a stroke. The narrowing of the blood vessels also makes it more difficult for blood to reach all parts of the body. This can lead to limb amputations for smokers.

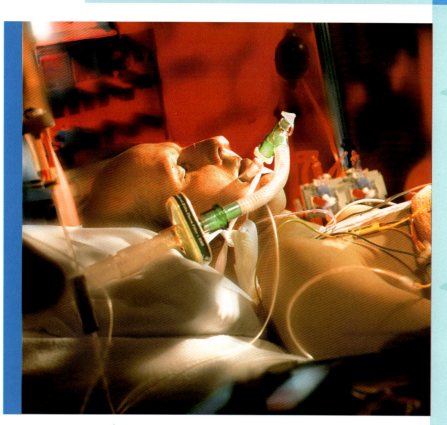

This man is breathing with the aid of a respirator after heart surgery. Smoking causes 25 per cent of heart disease deaths.

Lung health

Research the link between smoking and other lung diseases, such as emphysema and bronchitis.

It's your life

The younger someone is when they start to smoke, the more dangerous it is. Someone who begins to smoke at the age of 15 is three times more likely to die of cancer due to smoking than someone who starts in their mid-20s. This is partly because they are likely to smoke for longer but also smoking can damage the lungs of a teenager for ever, increasing the risk of lung cancer.

Smoking and sport

Smoking affects the lungs and breathing, making exercise increasingly difficult. As a result, it is unusual to find top athletes who smoke. Teenagers who are involved in sport are much less likely to take up smoking.

Sport and smoking do not go together. ▶

Less energy

When someone takes exercise their muscles require more oxygen, which is carried in the bloodstream. The lungs and heart need to work well in order to supply this oxygen, and to remove the waste product carbon dioxide from the body.

Yet the nicotine and carbon monoxide in cigarette smoke affect the blood and circulation, preventing some oxygen from reaching the muscles. The muscles have less energy and will tire more quickly. Still, a smoker who exercises regularly is likely to be in better health than a smoker who does not.

Sponsorship

Most large sporting events are funded by sponsors. For years, tobacco companies liked to support sport because it is watched by millions on TV and because it presents an image of adventure and success that they wanted to link with their cigarettes. In 2005 the European Union banned all tobacco-related sponsorship of sport because it believes that it encourages young smokers to take up the habit.

Your experience

"I rarely see our young players smoke. They are all aware of the health risks and none of them want to risk losing their place in the team by losing fitness."

U16 football coach

▲ A sports fan celebrates with a cigar.

Your view

Sponsorship deals mean more money for sport. Do you think that tobacco companies should be allowed to sponsor events?

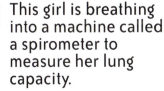

◄ This girl is breathing into a machine called a spirometer to measure her lung capacity.

Passive smoking

Breathing in other people's tobacco smoke is called 'passive smoking'. Anti-smoking groups have been concerned about the effects of passive smoking for over 30 years.

Health risks

Passive smokers are exposed to some of the risks faced by smokers themselves, including lung cancer and heart disease. Obviously the level of risk depends on the level of exposure to tobacco smoke.

This boy will breathe in his mother's smoke. ▼

Passive smoking and children

According to the World Health Organisation, almost half the world's children are exposed to other people's tobacco smoke. This raises their chance of developing asthma, bronchitis, middle-ear infections and pneumonia.

Pregnancy

Unborn children are also affected by passive smoking. If a woman smokes during pregnancy, she is likely to have a smaller than normal baby.

▼ Doctors advise against smoking during pregnancy.

Your experience

▶ "I suffer from asthma. My doctor says that asthma is caused by all sorts of things, but I know that if I go into a smoky room, I am much more likely to have an attack."

Jamal, aged 13

Public places

After a long and hard-fought campaign, anti-smoking campaigners have been rewarded with a ban on smoking in public places. In many countries, smoking is banned in offices, bars, restaurants, cinemas and other public buildings. The ban will help reduce deaths from passive smoking, particularly for those who work in bars and pubs.

Your view

▶ Pro-smoking campaigners argue that to ban smoking in public places is to deny smokers their rights. Anti-smokers demand the right to clean air. Whose rights do you think matter most and why?

▲ Smokers step outside to smoke.

The law

Many countries have laws to protect children from the dangers of smoking. Several countries have also passed laws stating that each packet of cigarettes must be clearly labelled with the nicotine and tar content, as well as carrying a strong health warning (see page 33).

Here a newsagent refuses to sell cigarettes to a teenager.

The law and young people

Many laws about smoking are intended to prevent young people from taking up the habit. In the UK and Australia, it is illegal for anyone to sell cigarettes to a person who appears to be under the age of 18. Shopkeepers can be fined large sums for breaking the law.

Taxes

Most countries tax the sale of tobacco, which means that an additional charge must be included in the price of every packet of cigarettes. This raises money for the government and helps to make it too expensive for people to afford to smoke.

Smuggling

Taxing cigarettes means that some people will try to avoid paying the tax. Smugglers illegally import cigarettes on which no tax is paid. They sell them at prices far below shop prices, whilst still making a huge

Your view

Many teenagers report that older people are happy to buy their cigarettes for them. Do you think they should? What could governments do to stop this from happening?

It's your life

Many governments try to stop people from smoking by making it more and more expensive. Yet many people continue to smoke despite the cost. Think of what smokers could do with the extra money if they gave up smoking.

profit for themselves. Aside from breaking the law, some of these smuggled cigarettes are likely to be bought by under-age smokers who won't be asked to prove they are over the age of 18.

Customs officials seize smuggled cigarettes and alcohol.

The costs of smoking

Apart from the cost to someone's health and the actual cost of buying cigarettes, smoking costs society as a whole. Smokers cause more fires, they take more time off work and they generally need to use health services more than non-smokers.

A doctor advises a patient on how to stop smoking.

Your experience

"I don't like to think how much money I've spent on cigarettes in the last year."
Megan, aged 19

An expensive habit

An average smoker probably spends £2,000 per year on cigarettes. If money is tight, that means less money to spend on food, clothes or having fun.

Health costs and taxes

In the UK the National Health Service spends close to £3 billion each year on treating the effects of smoking. Although the UK government receives around £9 billion in tax from the sale of cigarettes, this is still a great deal of money.

A young street boy in India.

Division of money spent on drug-related health problems.

- 22% alcohol
- 17% illegal drugs
- 61% smoking

Children's health

A study in Bangladesh has shown that poorer people who smoke spend less on food in order to pay for their habit. So their children lose out twice, with less food to eat and by breathing in their parents' smoke.

Smoking and the workplace

Smoking is expensive for employers. Smokers need to take far more days off work for illness over a lifetime than non-smokers. Smokers also take many more breaks at work so employers lose out on the number of hours that these employees work in a year.

Your view

Smokers point out that far more money is raised in taxes from the sale of cigarettes than is spent on treating smoking-related illness. Does that make it OK to smoke?

Advertising

Tobacco companies have spent billions advertising their products. When it was allowed, they placed adverts in magazines, on billboards, on TV and at cinemas. They sponsored events, offered free gifts and even paid to have their products smoked by celebrities.

The power of advertising

Tobacco adverts frequently linked smoking with stylish young people living a glamorous lifestyle. Although the tobacco companies always said that they aimed their advertising at adults, of course children saw the images. A good example of this was the mascot, Joe Camel, introduced in 1988, to promote Camel Light cigarettes. In 1992 a US medical report revealed that young children were more likely to recognise Joe Camel than Mickey Mouse! After several years of pressure, the company stopped using Joe Camel — but not until 1997.

The 'Joe Camel' mascot, used in adverts for Camel Lights (see above).

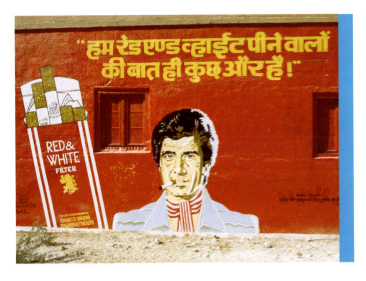

Your view

Anti-smoking campaigners now want to see smoking banned from films. Do you think this will stop people from taking up smoking?

Tobacco advertising on a wall in India. India banned tobacco advertising in 2004.

Changing times

Today many tobacco companies have entered into agreements with governments to control advertising. Tobacco advertising is hardly allowed in Europe, the USA and Australia, except in a small way in corner shops and newsagents. Tobacco companies moved on to promote smoking in Africa and Asia – but now some of the countries in these areas are starting to ban advertising.

Your view

Are you influenced by advertising? Tobacco companies say that they are aiming their adverts at adults. Do you think it is possible to limit advertising to one age group? What affects do adverts have on you?

Tobacco advertising on the door of a corner shop.

Tobacco companies

From its earliest days, the tobacco industry has made huge profits. It has often used these profits to protect its industry.

In Argentina this man's sunhat advertises Marlboro cigarettes.

The power of money

In the 1950s, when medical research began to prove the link between cancer and smoking, the tobacco industry in the USA started to fund its own research. Named the Tobacco Industry Research Council, it tried to cover up the damaging health effects of cigarette smoke. It also funded research to develop a 'healthier' cigarette. The industry proclaimed that adding filters and reducing the tar content in cigarettes would make them healthier. They also paid top lawyers to defend them if anyone accused them of not warning of the health dangers of smoking. At first they won these law cases but now some companies are paying out compensation to people damaged by cigarettes.

New markets

When the large tobacco companies in the USA and Europe realised that governments would continue to tighten controls on the sale of tobacco, they started to sell their products in more African, Asian and Russian countries. Many of these countries cannot afford to educate people about the dangers of smoking. Tobacco companies also have much more freedom to sponsor events and advertise their cigarettes in these areas of the world. Some countries are starting to bring in controls but most have not. Alongide a rise in levels of smoking is a rise in smoking-related diseases (see pages 18–19).

The World Health Organisation has noticed a big rise in the number of women who smoke worldwide.

Your view

Tobacco companies now fund campaigns to prevent young people from taking up smoking. They also give money to schemes that provide proof-of-age cards to young people, to make it more difficult for under-18s to buy cigarettes. Tobacco companies always stress that smoking is an adult's choice, like many other decisions in life. Does this argument work for you? What points can you think of that agree or disagree with this?

Cigarette production at a R.J. Reynolds factory in the USA.

Anti-smoking campaigns

Anti-smoking campaigns are usually organised by health services or anti-smoking pressure groups. Generally they aim to prevent young people from smoking, persuade smokers to quit and protect people from passive smoking.

Which ones work?

Different campaigns work for different groups of people. Governments use posters, TV adverts and official reports to get their message across. A recent television campaign showed children pleading with their parents to stop smoking.

School programmes

Most schools run anti-smoking sessions, yet many young people choose to ignore them. Researchers say this is because young people tend not to be worried about the long-term effects of smoking. So some recent campaigns have focused on less life-threatening problems, such as yellow teeth, bad breath and old-looking skin, to get their message across.

The film star, Jackie Chan, supports an anti-smoking rally in the USA.

Printed health warnings

Since the 1960s, a growing number of governments have forced cigarette manufacturers to print health warnings on their products. These vary from printed messages to colour photos of lung tumours, diseased hearts and rotting teeth. By law, the warnings must take up a large proportion of the space on the packaging.

Your experience

"I stopped smoking when my children started begging me to stop. They hated to think I might die."

Janine, aged 36

Smoking kills

Smoking harms your baby

Smoking makes you unattractive

Smoking is highly addictive — don't start

Smokers die younger

▲◀ Health warnings on cigarette packets are not easy to ignore.

Canada: a case study

Canada was the first country to introduce photographic health warnings in 2001. With frightening photos on cigarette packets, levels of smoking dropped dramatically, especially amongst the young.

Your view

Which type of anti-smoking message do you think works?

Smoking other drugs

Tobacco is not the only drug that people choose to smoke. However it is not against the law to smoke tobacco. Some people choose to smoke cannabis and crack cocaine. These drugs are against the law because governments have decided that they are dangerous to people's health and to society in general.

A smoker inhales on the cigarette he has made from cannabis and tobacco.

Cannabis

Cannabis is made from the dried leaves of the cannabis plant. Like tobacco, it is usually smoked. It makes people feel relaxed or even sleepy while some become giggly and happy. Although it can help some people cope with the pain of the illness multiple sclerosis, it is linked with mental health difficulties, including depression and psychosis. Since cannabis is usually mixed with tobacco and smoked without a filter, research suggests that smoking three cannabis cigarettes a day may be as bad for the heart and lungs as smoking 20 normal cigarettes.

Crack cocaine

Cocaine is a drug made from the coca plant. When heated in a pipe, crack cocaine can be breathed in. It makes people feel 'on top of the world' but it is highly addictive. Users can die from an overdose. The smoke can seriously harm the lungs and cause chest pains.

A man smokes crack cocaine with a small blowtorch.

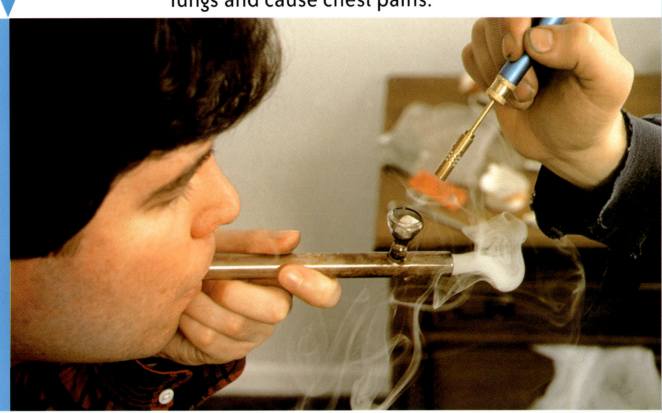

Your experience

"No one I know thinks cannabis is dangerous. Most of our parents smoked it when they were younger, didn't they?"

Michael, aged 15

Illegal drugs

Both cannabis and crack cocaine are illegal drugs. This means that it is illegal to buy, sell or carry either drug. If caught, the punishments range from a police warning to a prison sentence.

Giving up

Giving up smoking needs planning and determination. Because nicotine is so addictive, many smokers try to give up several times before they actually succeed. The lack of nicotine can make the ex-smoker feel restless, irritable and tired but there are lots of ways to help manage this.

Support

Once someone decides they want to stop smoking, it is vital that they get as much support from family and friends as possible. Some people prefer to go to a support group where they can share their experiences with people who understand what they are going through. Others try hypnosis or acupuncture, although experts argue about whether these treatments can help or not.

Support groups or counsellors can help people quit smoking.

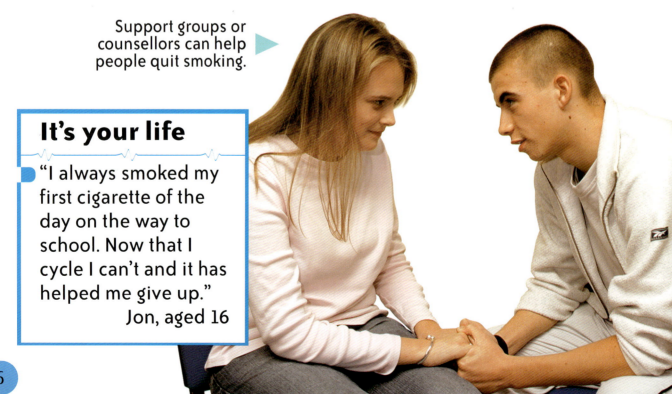

It's your life

"I always smoked my first cigarette of the day on the way to school. Now that I cycle I can't and it has helped me give up."
Jon, aged 16

Nicotine patches can help some people to quit smoking. ▶

Patches and gums

Nicotine patches and gums can help some people to stop smoking for good. These products release a small amount of nicotine into the body without the harmful effects of smoke on the lungs. The idea is to gradually reduce the use of the patches or chewing gum over a number of weeks until the user is free from dependence on nicotine altogether. Doctors can also prescribe drugs to help beat smoking.

Exercise

Taking exercise can be helpful because it releases feel-good chemicals into the brain that may help deal wth the effects of nicotine withdrawal.

Free help

There is so much help out there to help people stop smoking; support groups, one-to-one counsellors, trained advisors on the other end of the phone. A school nurse or doctor can help as well.

The good news!

Thousands of people do manage to stop smoking every day.

More good news

After only two days there is no nicotine left in the body. After one year the risk of a heart attack falls to about half that of a smoker.

◄ Giving up smoking gives people more energy.

Your experience

"I thought it would be easy to give up, but on the third day I got really bored and had a cigarette. The next time I tried I had an argument with my dad, and gave in again. This time I'm going to do it."

Carla, aged 17

Helpful hints for quitting

Avoid places and situations where you are more likely to smoke.

Tell people you are giving up so that they can offer support.

Make plans and keep busy so that you have less time to think about cigarettes. Take up a new hobby.

Ask your local nurse for advice

Health benefits

Whether you are helping someone to give up smoking or are giving up yourself, looking at this list might help:

Time since quitting	Health benefits
20 minutes	Blood pressure and pulse return to normal. Circulation improves.
8 hours	Levels of oxygen in the blood return to normal.
24 hours	There is no carbon monoxide or nicotine left in the body. Lungs start to clear out mucus.
1 month	The appearance of the skin improves.
3-9 months	Lungs clear themselves out, making breathing easier and releasing more energy.
1 year	Risk of a heart attack falls to half that of a smoker.

Your view

How would you help someone to give up smoking? What would stop you from smoking?

What would you rather spend your money on?

Think of the money!

Smoking costs a fortune. Smokers can save themselves so much money by giving up.

Making a choice

Smoking kills. Nicotine is one of the most addictive drugs. Although fewer and fewer people are choosing to take up smoking in the wealthier countries of the world, many people still ignore these two vital facts.

◀ We don't need to smoke if we want to have a good time.

It's your life

Can you say no?
No one can tell you what to do. In many areas of your life you have to make your own decisions about what to do and what not to do.

Looking cool

Smoking has long been linked with cool, young, attractive people. However, smoking actually ages the skin, makes the fingertips and teeth yellow, rots the gums and generally affects people's looks in a bad way.

Fitting in

Peer pressure can be very hard to resist. If your friends smoke, it is difficult not to join in. So if your friends have started smoking, it might be better to seek out different friends. If this is difficult, then some people tell their friends that they cannot smoke for health reasons, such as asthma.

Does smoking make you slim?

No. If this were true, all smokers would be slim! The nicotine in cigarettes can stop people from feeling hungry but smoking does not make people thin or lose weight.

It's your life

A hundred years ago, when people first started smoking, they did not know the health risks. Today that is not true. Now that you have read this book, will you ever smoke?

Many young smokers say they would prefer not to smoke.

It's your health!

If you are at an age where you are legally allowed to smoke, it is up to you to choose whether to smoke or not.

Have you made your choice?

Glossary

Acupuncture: inserting needles into the skin to treat pain or disease.

Addiction: a habit that is very hard to break.

Asthma: a health condition that affects the airways. During an asthma attack it can be difficult to breathe.

Blood pressure: the pressure of blood pressing against the blood vessels as it flows around the body.

Bronchitis: inflammation of the airways.

Cancer: a diseased growth in the body.

Cannabis: the dried leaves of the cannabis plant.

Carbon monoxide: poisonous gas present in tobacco smoke.

Circulation: the movement of the blood from the heart, to all areas of the body, and back to the heart.

Crack cocaine: smokeable form of the illegal drug cocaine.

Dopamine: a chemical released in the brain.

Emphysema: lung disease.

Filter: a mouthpiece that filters cigarette smoke.

Heart disease: all diseases of the heart and of the blood vessels supplying the heart.

Hypnosis: artificially produced sleep which can be used to guide someone's mind towards a desired outcome.

Native Americans: the people who were living in North and South America before European settlers arrived.

Nicotine: poisonous substance present in tobacco leaves.

Overdose: taking too much of a drug all at once.

Passive smoking: breathing in smoke from other people's cigarettes.

Pesticide: substance used to kill pests.

Psoriasis: skin disease.

Psychosis: a condition that affects the way a person thinks and feels.

Snuff: powdered tobacco.

Stroke: a serious medical condition that occurs when the blood supply to the brain is disturbed.

Tar: brown sticky substance found in cigarette smoke.

Tumour: a diseased growth in part of the body.

Withdrawal (from nicotine): feelings of anxiety, sleeplessness and irritability.

Further information

UNITED KINGDOM

Ask Doctor Ann

At the Website of a Teenage Health Freak you can ask Doctor Ann a question about smoking, or look at questions and answers on smoking.
www.doctorann.org/smoking/

NHS Smokefree

The National Health Service site dedicated to helping people to give up smoking.
http://smokefree.nhs.uk/

Quit because

The youth section of the UK charity Quit which helps people to give up smoking.
www.quitbecause.org.uk

The Site

Information about the effects of smoking.
www.thesite.org/drinkanddrugs/ smoking/givingupsmoking/smoking andhealthww.thesite.org/ drinkanddrugs

AUSTRALIA

Quit Now

The Australian National Tobacco Campaign offers information on smoking and health and gives tips on how to stop smoking.
www.quitnow.info.au/

OxyGen

OxyGen is packed with information about tobacco so that you can make your own decisions about smoking.
www.oxygen.org.au/

Children's Youth and Women's Health Service (South Australia)

This link will take you to the child and youth health part of the organisation's website.
www.cyh.com/Default.aspx?p=1

Note to parents and teachers: Every effort has been made by the Publishers to ensure that these websites are suitable for children, that they are of the highest educational value, and that they contain no inappropriate or offensive material. However, because of the nature of the Internet, it is impossible to guarantee that the contents of these sites will not be altered. We strongly advise that Internet access is supervised by a responsible adult.

Index

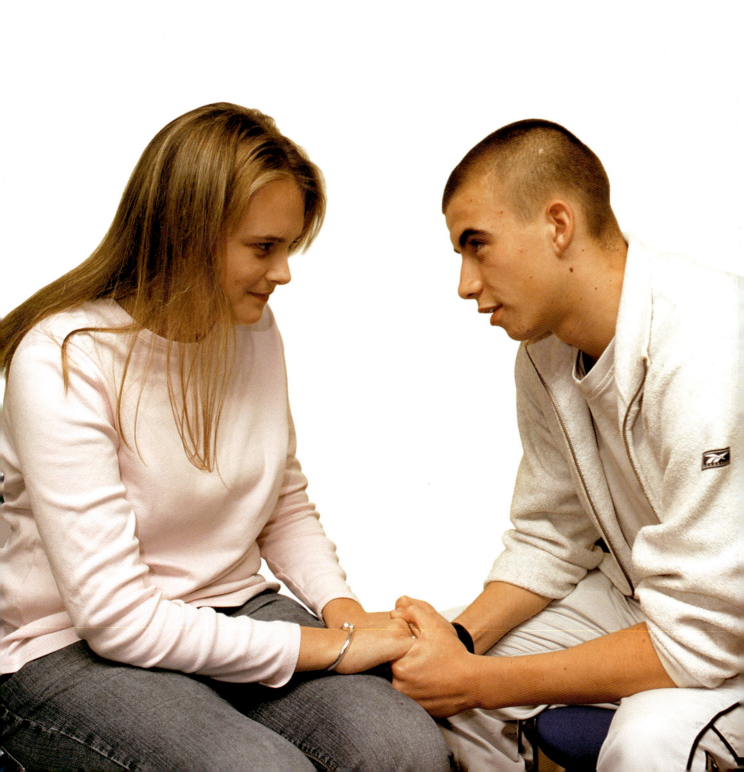